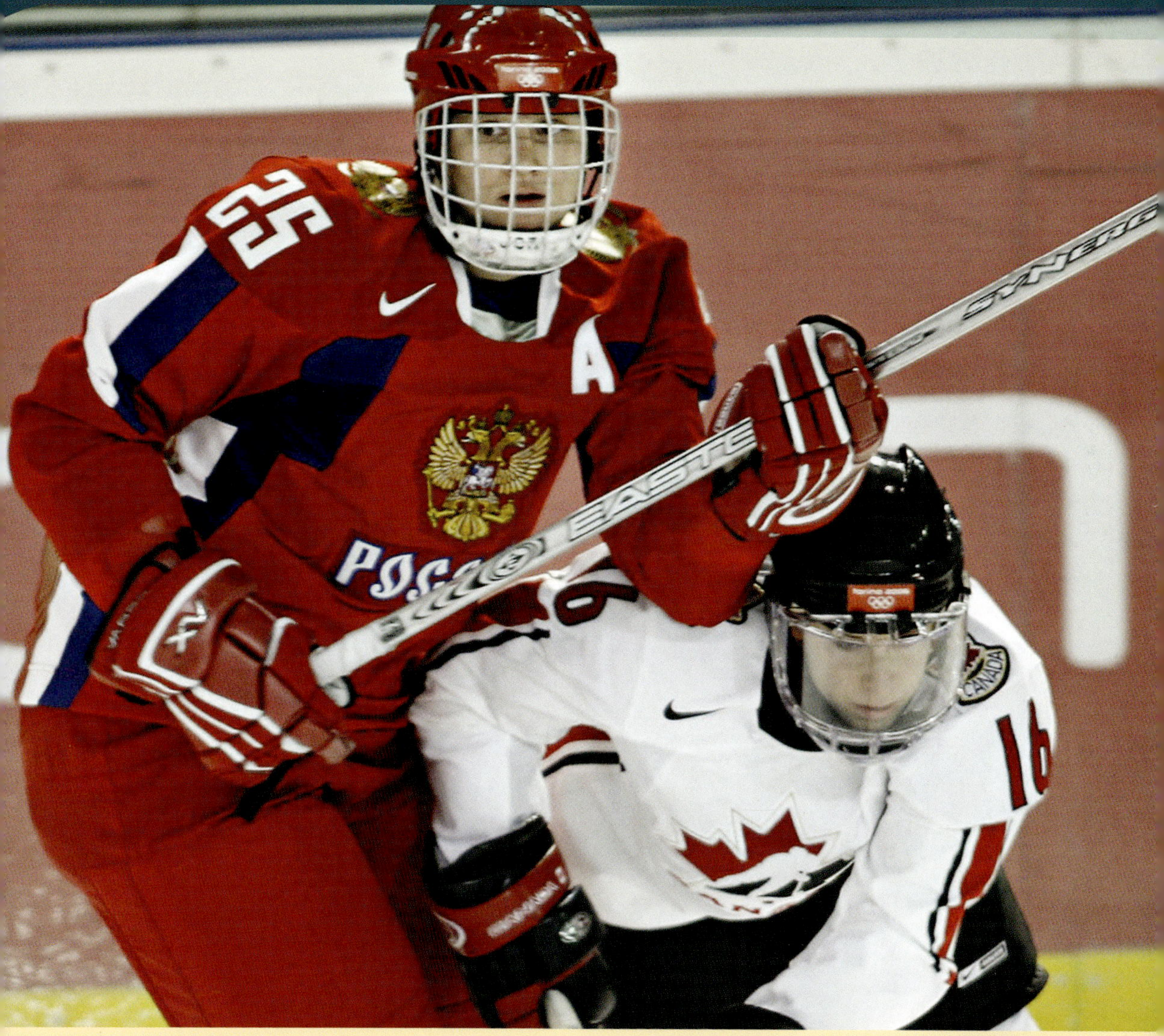

WHAT IT TAKES TO BE A PRO
HOCKEY PLAYER

by Kaitlyn Duling

www.12StoryLibrary.com

Copyright © 2020 by 12-Story Library, Mankato, MN 56002. All rights reserved. No part of this book may be reproduced or utilized in any form or by any means without written permission from the publisher.

12-Story Library is an imprint of Bookstaves.

Photographs ©: Ryan Remiorz/Associated Press, cover, 1; Matthew Jacques/Shutterstock.com, 4; Michael Miller/CC4.0, 5; Sergei Bachlakov/Shutterstock.com, 5; Krm500/CC2.0, 6; MaraZe/Shutterstock.com, 6; Pukhov K/Shutterstock.com, 7; William Notman & Son/PD, 8; StockphotoVideo/Shutterstock.com, 9; National Hockey League/PD, 9; Lucky Business/Shutterstock.com, 10; Lorraine Swanson/Shutterstock.com, 11; Michael Miller/CC4.0, 12; Leonard Zhukovsky/Shutterstock.com, 13; Northwest/CC4.0, 14; BDZ Sports/CC4.0, 15; Michael Miller/CC4.0, 16; Gints Ivuskans/Shutterstock.com, 17; antoniodiaz/Shutterstock.com, 18; Jacob Lund/Shutterstock.com, 19; Ivica Drusany/Shutterstock.com, 20; MarinaKo/Shutterstock.com, 21; Alex Goykhman/CC4.0, 22; Kiev.Victor/Shutterstock.com, 23; Eddie Collins/CC3.0, 24; Hakandahlstrom/CC3.0, 25; TheAHL/CC2.0, 26; EJ Hersom/US Military, 27; Derek Jensen/PD, 28; Zamboni Company/PD, 29; Counselman Collection from McClure/CC2.0, 29

ISBN
9781632357625 (hardcover)
9781632358714 (paperback)
9781645820451 (ebook)

Library of Congress Control Number: 2019938691

Printed in the United States of America
July 2019

About the Cover
Canada's Janya Hefford (16) tries to get around Russia's Ekaterina Pashkevich during the Winter Olympics in 2006.

Access free, up-to-date content on this topic plus a full digital version of this book. Scan the QR code on page 31 or use your school's login at 12StoryLibrary.com.

Table of Contents

Life as a Hockey Pro: The Real Story 4

A Day in the Life 6

A Brief History of the Game 8

Leagues and Schools 10

Juniors or College? 12

The Draft 14

Agents and Contracts 16

Staying in Top Shape 18

Taking a Risk 20

The Stanley Cup 22

After the Game 24

Doing Good and Giving Back 26

Fun Facts about Hockey 28

Glossary 30

Read More 31

Index 32

About the Author 32

Life as a Hockey Pro: The Real Story

Life on the ice sounds pretty cool. Zooming by on skates. Listening to the roar of the crowd. Slapping the puck into the net. Yes, hockey is exciting. The pros who get to play it are lucky.

Hockey is popular in countries with cold climates. The United States, Canada, and some European countries have loved hockey for a long time. Hockey has its own stars, like Canadian centerman Sidney Crosby, nicknamed "Sid the Kid." In 2007, he became the youngest team captain in the National Hockey League (NHL). He captains the Pittsburgh Penguins. Russian winger Alexander Ovechkin is another of today's best players.

The stars earn big salaries. They wear bright uniforms. They fight for gold medals at the Olympics. They practice, practice, practice. For the eight months of the pro season, players don't take days off, weekends, or vacations. They are constantly in the arena. They play 82 games each season.

Injuries are part of pro hockey life, too. Players fight. They fall. Sometimes they lose teeth. They are regulars at the doctor's office. When it comes to hockey, the pros are all-in.

> Pro hockey players practice almost every day during the season.

Canadian centerman Sidney Crosby in 2018.

WHO PLAYS PRO HOCKEY?

Hockey is popular in the United States. But most of the pros come from Canada. That's where pro hockey got its start. Canadians usually make up at about 45 percent of the National Hockey League, North America's pro league. US-born players make up around 25 percent. Other players come from Europe.

31
Number of teams in the NHL

- The league was formed in 1917 by five Canadian teams.
- The Montreal Canadiens were one of the first teams. They have won more championships than any other team.
- The league's 32nd team will start play in 2021. They will play in Seattle, Washington.

2

A Day in the Life

Swedish goalie Henrik Lundqvist.

Pros usually practice in the late morning. They have a team meeting. They eat snacks. Then they warm up. Practice includes plenty of drills on the ice. After practice, everyone eats lunch. Eating is an important routine. Food gives players energy for practice and games. Swedish goalie Henrik Lundqvist likes to eat spaghetti with meat sauce before he goes on the ice.

A pro hockey player's day is all about routine. With so many games in a season, it's important to have a regular schedule. Players sleep for 8 to 10 hours a night. This gives them energy for games. Many players take naps between practices and games. They need all the sleep they can get.

6

Travel is a way of life. Teams take buses and airplanes. Some fly on private jets. They eat meals on the plane. There is time to review games. There might be time for a nap, too.

On game days, players arrive early at the rink. They eat and tape up their hockey sticks. Some get massages or talk to coaches. After a 20-minute warm-up, the players are ready.

The team will win or lose. Either way, they meet afterward to review the game. There is time to talk to the media. Then they eat a large dinner and go home or to their hotel to sleep. Tomorrow is another day.

5
Swedish winger Carl Hagelin's age when he became a soccer fan

- Hagelin follows soccer in his downtime.
- While traveling with his team, he has time to play soccer video games.
- Hagelin's speed makes him one of the top players in the NHL. In 2012, he won the NHL Fastest Skater competition.

It's important to warm up before a game.

A Brief History of the Game

Many people think of hockey as a Canadian sport. This is partly true. The ice hockey we know today started in Canada in the 1800s. Before that came field hockey and lacrosse. These sports are thousands of years old. The earliest people played sports with sticks, goals, and balls. Two things make hockey different. It is played on ice, and it is played with a puck.

Hockey-like games on ice began in England. A hockey-like game was also played by indigenous people in Canada. It was played with a square wooden block instead of a ball. This game may have been influenced by the Irish.

Yes, ice hockey flourished in Canada. But its roots are global.

The first organized hockey game was played in 1875 in Montreal. By the late 1800s, hockey was popular in Canada. It eventually spread across North America and Europe. In 1910, the National Hockey Association was formed.

An indoor hockey game in Montreal, Canada, in 1893.

This would later turn into the National Hockey League (NHL). The NHL is the premier pro league today. The National Women's Hockey League was founded in 2015.

1915
Year when fighting was listed as a foul in the national hockey rule book

- During the 2018–19 NHL season, Canadian winger Evander Kane received the most penalties. He had 47.
- When a player receives a penalty, he gets two minutes in the penalty box.
- One of the most common reasons for a penalty is high-sticking.

A BRUTAL SPORT

The first public indoor hockey game took place in 1875. Benches were smashed and heads punched. The game's most violent days were in the early 1900s. During those years, several players died from in-game injuries. Today the game is still violent. Fans often watch fights and see injuries.

4

Leagues and Schools

Pro hockey players are often young. Especially rookies. Finnish center Jesperi Kotkaniemi played his first pro game when he was 17 years old. He joined the NHL at 18. He is a strong player. Players like Kotkaniemi start skating in childhood.

Children can start hockey at age four or five. They might join youth leagues in their hometowns. Local rinks offer teams grouped by age. Over the last decade, eight-and-under hockey has grown. Over 100,000 kids under age eight sign up across the United States each year.

6
Number of players on each side during a hockey game

- Each side is three forwards, two defensive players, and a goalie. Each team has four lines of forwards and two lines of defensive players. The lines take turns playing.
- A pro team can have up to 20 players during a game.
- Teams usually have five or more coaches. One coach focuses on the goalies.

Hockey camps and clinics help players improve their game.

To get practice, kids go to camps. Some NHL teams offer camps and clinics. They can last hours, days, or weeks. American forward Hannah Brandt hosts her own hockey camp for girls. In places with long winters, kids can practice outdoors. Ponds and lakes freeze. People make their own backyard rinks.

Children join school teams, too. Hockey is offered in many middle schools and high schools. Some kids even go to boarding school to play hockey. A good team can make a player even stronger.

TRAVEL TEAMS

Some young hockey players join travel teams. These teams have tryouts. The tryouts are competitive. Teams travel for games. Sometimes they play teams in other states. Playing on a travel team can be expensive, but it is a good way to gain skills. Players also make friends from outside their own school and hometown.

11

5

Juniors or College?

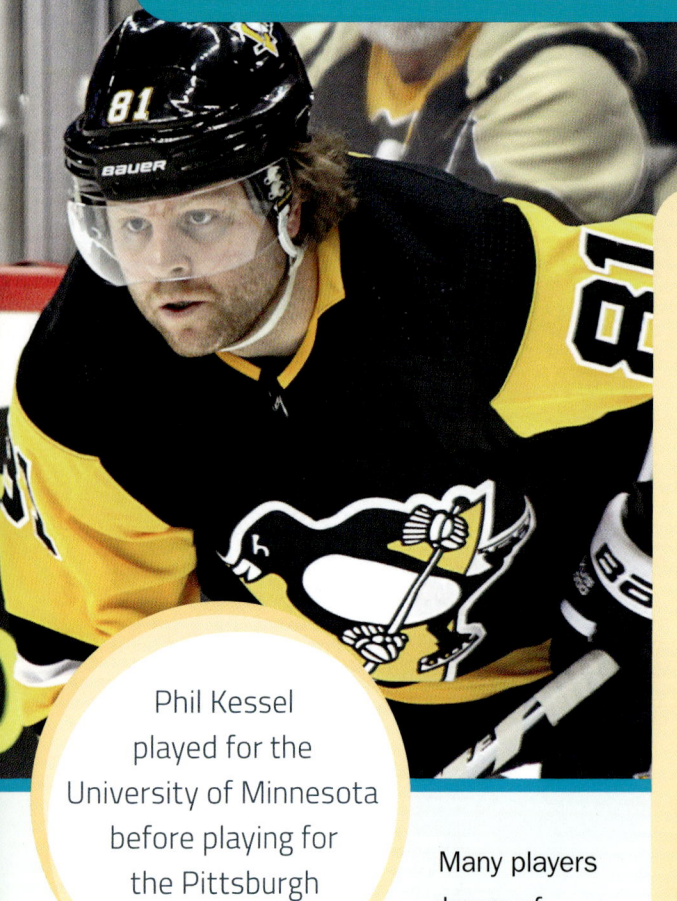

Phil Kessel played for the University of Minnesota before playing for the Pittsburgh Penguins.

Many players dream of going pro. How do they do it? It takes years of hard work and practice. When a player is a teenager, he or she has two options.

One option is college. There are many college hockey teams in

30%
NHL players who went to college for at least one hockey season

- Many players work hard to finish their college degrees. Some take online classes or go back to school after retiring from the NHL.
- American winger Ryan Donato finished up his junior year at Harvard while playing for the Boston Bruins. Sometimes he had games and classes back-to-back.
- College hockey coaches are required to have a bachelor's degree. American defenseman Brooks Orpik wants to coach one day, so he took night classes during the summer.

the United States and Canada. There are some in other countries, too. Players earn their college degree while playing for a team. Most US college hockey programs are in the north and northeast part of the country. American winger Phil Kessel played for the University of Minnesota. Then he played for the Pittsburgh Penguins, an NHL team.

College players balance school and sports. Some players decide to skip college. Teens can choose to enter the junior leagues instead. The juniors are for players ages 16 to 20. These teams help train players for a possible pro career. Junior leagues have multiple levels. If players do well, they might get drafted to the NHL. In Canada, many players get drafted from Major Junior leagues. This is the top level of amateur hockey there.

SIZE MATTERS

Hockey players must be strong and fast. Many recruiters look for players who are large. Hockey is a physical game. A player's body takes hits. It blocks shots. Players who are tall and heavy make great defensemen. Long arms help, too. In hockey, bigger tends to be better.

Ryan Donato at the Winter Olympics in 2018.

13

6

The Draft

Some players return to hockey each season. Others retire. Teams need new players if they want to improve. They add new players through a draft. The NHL draft occurs over two days each June. It is held in a different location every year. Male players ages 18 to 20 can participate. Players from outside North America can be up to 21 years old. The best players in college and the junior leagues are considered top picks.

The 2019 NHL draft took place at the Rogers Arena in Vancouver, Canada.

Usually 14 teams get picks. Only teams that didn't go to the playoffs get to attend the draft.

Teams take turns choosing players. Teams with the fewest wins over the last season get to pick first. There are seven rounds. Teams pick multiple times. A drawing decides the order in which the teams will pick. The NHL uses a lottery ball machine. The event is broadcast on TV and streamed online. Many fans watch and wait. They want to know which players will join their favorite teams.

14

The Buffalo Beauts won the Isobel Cup in 2017.

5%
Chance a college or junior player has of making it to the NHL

- Each NHL team can have 50 signed players at a time. Only 20 can suit up for a game.
- The NWHL has its own draft in June. Female players are drafted out of college.
- The first NHL draft, held in 1963, was more like a private league meeting. The event went public in 1980.

WHAT ABOUT WOMEN?

Female players go pro, too. The NWHL has five teams. They play a championship each year. It is called the Isobel Cup. Over the years, the female pros have grown frustrated. The players only earn a few thousand dollars a year. Most have full-time jobs in addition to hockey. Also, women's pro hockey doesn't provide health insurance, even though the sport can be dangerous. Unless it finds a way to support its players, the NWHL may not last in its current form.

7

Agents and Contracts

John Tavares played for the New York Islanders before landing a contract with the Toronto Maple Leafs.

To get to the pros, players need agents. An agent represents a player. He or she talks to the player, then the teams. The talks go back and forth. Agents help players negotiate. They discuss money, schedules, and contracts. An agent usually earns a percentage of a player's salary. The higher the salary, the more the agent earns.

Even young players get agents. An agent can help a player find a junior or college team. Canadian center John Tavares has a great agent. Pat Brisson helped Tavares score a big contract with the Toronto Maple Leafs. Tavares will make $11 million a year for seven years.

Contracts are agreements between players and teams. The player agrees to play for a specific team. A contract includes the player's salary. It includes bonus money he might receive for signing early. It says how long the player will be connected to the team. A contract can last for many years.

Canadian center Connor McDavid earns a good salary. But he makes even more money from

$650,000
Minimum wage an NHL player can earn in a year

- Each team has a salary cap. This is the total amount of money they can spend on players.
- NHL players receive their salaries whether they play games or not. Some sit out due to injuries.
- Most players in the NWHL make between $5,000 and $7,000.

endorsements. McDavid is paid to support brands and companies. He has a contract with Adidas, among others.

Connor McDavid (97), of the Edmonton Oilers, also earns money from endorsements.

8

Staying in Top Shape

Pro hockey players are some of the best athletes in the world. They are strong. They are fast skaters. They are in top shape. They must be—hockey season is long.

The regular season runs from October to April. Then the best teams enter the postseason. The playoffs run from May to June. The Stanley Cup Playoffs are usually in early June. After that, the players enter the off season. But they don't really have time off. Players stay in shape all summer and fall. When it is time to play again, they are ready.

Players work out in a variety of ways. Many players lift weights. They need to have strong muscles. They practice skating. Some run. Players practice their agility, too. American defenseman Connor Carrick does agility drills. He runs through a

Box jumps help build strength and balance.

Running on sand improves balance and agility.

ladder on the floor. This improves his skating skills.

Canadian-American defenseman Jakob Chychrun does box jumps. He sits on a stool in front of a box. Then he quickly stands, swings his arms, and jumps on top of the box. This builds strength and balance. Both are important in pro hockey.

Canadian center Nic Petan works out on the beach. Running on sand is hard. His muscles get stronger. His balance gets better. It might sound strange, but beach workouts help keep Petan fit for the pros. The ocean views don't hurt either.

8
Number of months the NHL season lasts

- Canadian winger Patrick Marleau has played over 1,600 games in his career.
- At 42 years old, American center Matt Cullen is the oldest active player in the NHL.
- Cullen went pro in 1996. He's played over 1,500 games.

THINK ABOUT IT
Pro hockey players eat, sleep, and breathe hockey. Do you have a hobby you love that much?

9

Taking a Risk

Hockey is a rough, tough, aggressive game. Injuries are common, especially at the pro level. Players get hit with sticks. They get into fights on the ice. Their bodies slam into each other. Sometimes they fall. In the worst cases, players have been cut by skates. The blades are sharp and dangerous.

Players collide on the ice. Wham! Collarbones break. Joints get torn.

Teeth are knocked out. Players take hits to the head from sticks, walls, pucks, and punches. They can suffer concussions. These are brain injuries. When players are seriously hurt, they sit out.

Hockey gear is key. Players wear rigid but flexible helmets, sometimes with visors or face cages. They wear shoulder pads, elbow pads, and shin guards.

Even with protective hockey gear, players can still get injured.

$185
Cost of a single NHL hockey stick

- Each player goes through 60 to 125 sticks a year.
- Players can choose their hockey sticks. Czech winger David Pastrnak designed his own custom stick. It features a drawing of the Boston skyline. It even has an emoji on the handle.
- The first hockey sticks were made of wood. Today, most sticks are made of composites like fiberglass. They are increasingly light, strong, and flexible.

Mouth guards protect their teeth. They were padded gloves and padded shorts.

Canadian defenseman Vince Dunn got hurt at the worst time. His team was headed to the 2019 Stanley Cup. Then a puck flew at his face. It hit him in the mouth. In hockey, you never know when an injury might happen.

Pucks fly at goalies. The goalies block them with their bodies. They wear special catching gloves and huge leg pads. Add a chest protector, neck protector, helmet, and face mask. A goalie's outfit can cost up to $55,000 per season.

21

10

The Stanley Cup

Each June, the best teams in the NHL go head-to-head. They all want to win the Stanley Cup. The Cup is over 125 years old. It was donated by Sir Frederick Arthur Stanley in 1892. He presented it to the top hockey team in Canada. The NHL has owned the Cup since 1926.

The Stanley Cup trophy is kept by the winning team for a year.

Made of silver and nickel, the Cup is huge. Winners have their team names inscribed on the trophy. It stands 35.25 inches (89.54 cm) tall. It weighs 34.5 pounds (15.5 kg). When a team wins the Stanley Cup Final, they are the best in the NHL. They get to keep the Cup for an entire year.

The players share their trophy. Each player on the winning team gets to have the Cup for one day. American

The Hockey Hall of Fame in Toronto, Ontario, Canada.

24
Number of times the Montreal Canadiens have won the Stanley Cup

- The Toronto Maple Leafs have won 13 Stanley Cups, putting them in second place.
- The Stanley Cup Final has only been cancelled twice. The first time was in 1919 due to an outbreak of the flu.
- The whole 2004–05 NHL season was cancelled due to a disagreement over players' salaries.

center Nick Bonino ate his mom's spaghetti out of the Cup. American winger Phil Bourque went swimming with it.

HALL OF FAMERS

The Hockey Hall of Fame is in Toronto, Ontario, Canada. It holds the history of ice hockey. It also honors great players and coaches. Players must retire from the sport before they can be honored. The Hall of Fame opened in 1943. Nearly 300 players have been inducted. Six are women. Canadian winger Jayna Hefford was inducted in 2018.

11

After the Game

A pro career doesn't last forever. The average pro hockey player is active for about five years. After that, players move on. They find other jobs. Some still work in hockey. They become agents or coaches. Some become scouts. American center Scott Gomez became an NHL coach after playing in the league for over 15 years.

Some pro hockey players skipped college and went straight to the pros. After the NHL, they might go back to school. Others pursue careers that don't require degrees. Canadian center John Cullen now works at a car dealership. American winger Sean Avery became a model. Canadian goalie Clint Malarchuk became a veterinary tech and a horse dentist.

Many NHL players aren't from the United States or Canada. When their time in the NHL is done, some return to their home countries. There, they can play for the national

NHL player Sean Avery pursued a career in modeling after playing professional hockey.

Wayne Gretzky in 1997.

894
Number of goals Canadian center Wayne Gretzky scored during his career

- Gretzky remains the top scorer in the history of the NHL. He played from 1978 to 1999.
- Many people consider Gretzky the greatest hockey player of all time. His nickname is "The Great One."
- Gretzky holds the record for most goals scored during a season: 92.

team or in a pro league. Canadian-American center Mike Fisher took another route. Instead of a job or hobby, he pursued love. He married country music superstar Carrie Underwood.

THINK ABOUT IT
If you could meet a pro hockey player, what would you ask him or her?

25

12

Doing Good and Giving Back

Men's pro hockey players can make millions of dollars. How do they spend it? Many players give away a portion of their salary. They also give something else of value—their time. Hockey players are celebrities. When they show up for a cause, people come to see them.

Hockey Fights Cancer is an NHL organization that supports cancer patients. Players and teams have charity nights. They wear lavender jerseys and lavender stick tape to support the cause.

As a team, the Montreal Canadiens help build ice rinks around their city. They give millions of dollars to people in need. They visit children's hospitals.

Each year, the King Clancy Memorial Trophy goes to a hockey player who is committed to his community. The award includes $25,000 for charity. Canadian winger Brendan Shanahan won the trophy in 2003. He started a smoke detector collection. Since then, his program has collected more than 30,000 smoke detectors. The Detroit Red Wings donate them throughout the state of Michigan.

The NHL also sponsors Hockey Is for Everyone. They aim to make hockey

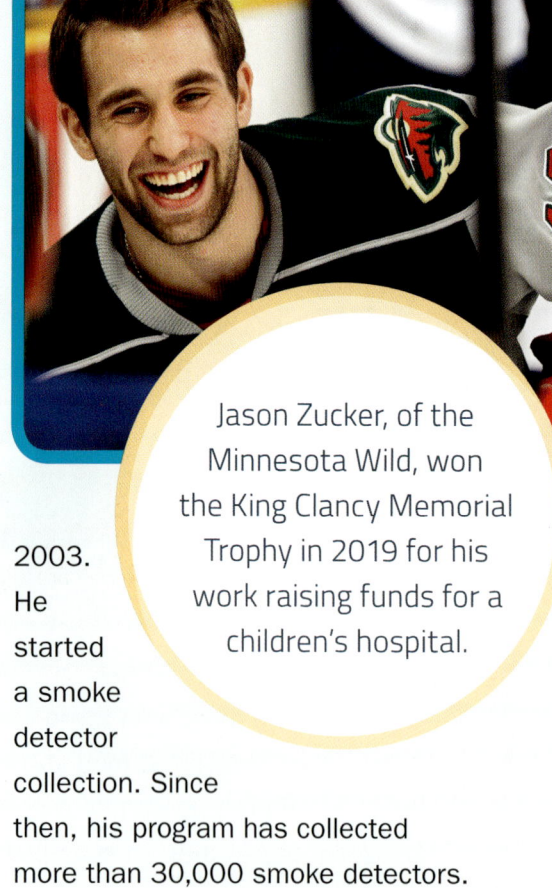

Jason Zucker, of the Minnesota Wild, won the King Clancy Memorial Trophy in 2019 for his work raising funds for a children's hospital.

26

7
Number of USA Warriors teams

- Warrior teams are made up of wounded US veterans.
- A sled hockey team is available. Players sit on a sled with two blades. They carry two sticks and use them to propel themselves across the ice.
- The Congressional Hockey Challenge is an annual charity game that supports USA Warriors Hockey. Federal lawmakers and staff members play in an NHL arena.

a safe and welcoming sport for all. They support LGBTQ players, black players, female players, and many other groups.

Players who give back are real hockey heroes both on and off the ice.

THINK ABOUT IT
If you made millions of dollars as a pro hockey player, what would you do to give back?

US Air Force Senior Airman Nikole Sweeney scores a goal at the Warriors Games.

Fun Facts about Hockey

- During the 2017–18 seasons, 23,692,327 fans attended NHL games. Each regular NHL season has 1,271 games. This means about 18,600 fans attended each game.

- The Bell Center in Montreal, Canada, is the biggest hockey arena in the world. It can hold over 21,000 fans. The Montreal Canadiens have won many matches on their home ice.

- The Pittsburgh Penguins used to play in an arena called the Igloo. The San Jose Sharks nicknamed their arena the Shark Tank.

The Mellon Arena, in Pittsburgh, Pennsylvania, was nicknamed the Igloo. It was demolished in 2012.

- A Zamboni is a special machine used in hockey arenas. It resurfaces ice, making it smooth. The Zamboni was invented in 1949.

- The rubber hockey pucks used in NHL games are one inch (2.54 cm) high. Each puck weighs six ounces (170 g). Pucks are frozen before play. This keeps them from bouncing on the ice. A typical NHL game uses 40 to 45 pucks. A puck can fly across the ice (or through the air) at speeds up to 100 miles per hour (160 km/hr).

- Whenever the Detroit Red Wings are in the playoffs, you can expect to see an octopus. According to Detroit legend, the tradition started in 1952. A fish market owner tossed an octopus onto the ice during a game. He thought the animal's eight legs would help the team win eight games. Today fans still keep up the tradition. They sneak frozen octopi into the arena and hurl them onto the ice.

- The Stanley Cup is full of engraved names. There are over 2,200 names in all. The Cup is also full of errors. Boston is misspelled as "Bqstqn." The Toronto Maple Leafs are written as the "Leaes." Canadian winger Adam Deadmarsh appeared on the trophy, but his name was misspelled. It said "Adam Deadmarch." That error was eventually corrected.

The Zamboni was invented in 1949 by Frank Zamboni, the son of Italian immigrants.

Glossary

agility
The ability to move quickly, easily, and gracefully.

competitive
Situations in which some people are trying hard to be better or more successful than others.

concussions
Injuries to the brain caused by hard hits or blows to the head.

drafted
In sports, the process of being chosen to be on a pro team.

drills
Repeated practice of one movement or skill.

endorsements
Public, often paid, support of certain brands, products, and companies.

high-sticking
Hitting an opponent on or above the shoulders with the hockey stick.

media
Means of mass communication, including TV, radio, the internet, apps, magazines, and more.

postseason
The end of the regular season and the beginning of games that determine a champion.

rookies
New players in the pro league.

scouts
In sports, people who travel to watch up-and-coming players. Scouts determine if a player will be a good fit for a team.

team captain
The player that leads his or her teammates.

winger
In hockey, a forward who plays along the outer area of the ice. The position is either left wing or right wing.

Read More

Hewson, Anthony K. *US Women's Hockey Team*. Minneapolis, MN: ABDO, 2019.

Martin, Brett S. *STEM in Hockey*. Minneapolis, MN: ABDO, 2018.

Monson, James. *Behind the Scenes Hockey*. Minneapolis, MN: Lerner Publishing Group, 2020.

Nicks, Erin. *Behind the Scenes of Pro Hockey*. Mankato, MN: Capstone, 2019.

Visit 12StoryLibrary.com

Scan the code or use your school's login at **12StoryLibrary.com** for recent updates about this topic and a full digital version of this book. Enjoy free access to:

- Digital ebook
- Breaking news updates
- Live content feeds
- Videos, interactive maps, and graphics
- Additional web resources

Note to educators: Visit 12StoryLibrary.com/register to sign up for free premium website access. Enjoy live content plus a full digital version of every 12-Story Library book you own for every student at your school.

Index

agents, 16-17
Avery, Sean, 24

camps, 11
careers after hockey, 24
charities, 26-27
Clancy Memorial Trophy, 26
college teams, 12-13, 14-15
Crosby, Sidney, 4-5

Donato, Ryan, 12-13

gear, 20-21
Gretzky, Wayne, 25

Hagelin, Carl, 7
history, 8-9, 23
Hockey Hall of Fame, 23

injuries, 4, 9, 20

junior leagues, 13, 14-15

Kessel, Phil, 12-13

Lundqvist, Henrik, 6

McDavid, Connor, 17

National Women's Hockey League (NWHL), 15, 17

NHL draft, 14-15

penalties, 9
practice, 4, 6, 11, 18

salaries, 16-17, 23, 26
Stanley Cup, 22-23

Tavares, John, 16
travel, 6-7, 11

Warrior teams, 27
workouts, 18-19

youth leagues, 10-11

About the Author

Kaitlyn Duling has written over 60 books for children and teens. She loves to learn about sports. Kaitlyn lives in Washington, DC, where she roots for the Washington Capitals.

READ MORE FROM 12-STORY LIBRARY

Every 12-Story Library Book is available in many fomats. For more information, visit **12StoryLibrary.com**